Introduction

The castle with the millpond in the foreground and the dam on the right

*"An oulde ruynous Castle walled about,
and in forme not much unlyke a shield
hanging with one poynt upwarde ..."*
(WILLIAM STOCKDALE, 1586)

Prudhoe Castle "attains more nearly to
the ideal of a Border castle than does any
other in Northumberland," wrote C J
Bates in 1891. Others may have their
own favourites but those travelling by
road or rail along the Tyne Valley cannot
but be impressed by the castle's situation
on the tree-covered bluff, its strategic
position and grandly standing ruins.

Like most Northumbrian castles, apart
from coastal ones such as Bamburgh and
Dunstanburgh, Prudhoe is close to a
river. It is the third major castle along the
Tyne, after Tynemouth and Newcastle as
one proceeds upstream, and it
commands the river crossing at
Ovingham as well as the west–east road
from Carlisle to Newcastle. It also stands
close to the junction of that road with the

Roman road of Dere Street at Corbridge
which continues northeast through
Redesdale across the Cheviots at Carter
Bar to Jedburgh. The castle looked north
towards one of the Scottish invasion
routes.

Prudhoe Castle commands a fertile
stretch of the Tyne valley and this
provided the economic basis for the
barony of Prudhoe. The comparative
wealth of the immediate region at an
even earlier period before the Norman
Conquest is demonstrated by the
sculptured crosses and Anglo-Saxon west
tower of Ovingham church, in the parish
of which Prudhoe originally lay.
Excavations inside the castle have shown
that beneath the outer ward was a
defended enclosure containing traces of
timber buildings probably belonging to
the mid-eleventh century.

The castle is set on the end of a steep-
sided spur, the summit of which is about
150 feet (46m) above the river. The site

3

was carefully chosen to make the best use of natural defences which additionally were formed by streams that had cut deep denes on either side of the spur. These were improved to create formidable defensive ditches and ramparts. Inside these is the massive earthwork enclosure of the inner castle on which stand the masonry towers and curtain walls.

Prudhoe's history is principally associated with two of the most prominent Northumbrian families—first, the Umfravilles, originating from Normandy, who were firmly established here by Henry I; then, when the male line of the Prudhoe Umfravilles failed, the barony came into the hands of the Percys through marriage in 1398. The castle is still owned by the Duke of Northumberland, though at present it is managed by English Heritage on behalf of the Department of National Heritage.

Although the castle first appears in the historical records quite late in the twelfth century, archaeological research has shown that an early defended enclosure developed into a substantial fortification following the Norman Conquest and thereafter. The castle later played an active part in the intermittent warfare between Scottish and English kings and was besieged several times. The sieges of 1173 and 1174 by William the Lion of Scotland were recorded in the chronicle of Jordan Fantosme, who wrote as a contemporary eyewitness, and whose account is claimed to provide a rare insight into the nature of medieval warfare.

Castles, however, were not simply fortresses, and as the place which served as the head of a barony, Prudhoe would have been an important administrative centre. It was clearly also an aristocratic residence of some elaboration and magnificence, which continued to be improved during the later middle ages and into the sixteenth century. A survey of the castle was compiled by William Stockdale in 1586 and this is a very helpful description of the castle before it fell out of use.

Although parts of the castle were to fall into decay and ruin during the seventeenth century, continuing use and occupation were maintained. The castle was the home of the duke's agent for the upper Tyne. Even today there is a custodian maintaining residential continuity.

Repairs and a radical reordering of the castle were carried out in the early years of the nineteenth century by the Duke of Northumberland. Indeed, the changing practices and standards of historic conservation can be followed at Prudhoe and are of some interest in themselves. The construction of the Georgian house, now termed the Manor House, on the site of a medieval residential cross-range dividing the enclosure into two parts, is a dominating feature. While strongly contributing to the castle's architectural development, its construction and the contemporary repairs to the surviving ruins have obscured evidence which might help us understand the successive stages and form of the castle's domestic development in the area between the medieval cross range and the Great Tower. The Manor House does, however, repeat a strong visual element separating the wards—the private from the more public portions of the castle. The removal of the ruined buildings in the inner ward at the same time as the building of the Manor House was also coupled with the consolidation of the great tower. This was, in the words of C F Bates, "at the time of fortunate repairs and unfortunate alterations in order to secure the monotonous symmetry then in vogue."

Descriptive Tour

Aerial view of the castle, looking northeast. Compare this with the plan on the centre pages

The first defences consisted of earth ramparts and timber walls and palisades. When seen in plan, the shape of the later walled castle suggests that originally there were two distinct enclosures joined as if in a rough figure of eight. In the castle's later form, the inner ward (courtyard or bailey) contained the great tower (keep) at its centre and the outer ward was entered from the present gatehouse.

The tour begins in the outer ward (**1** on the plan on the centre pages), to the east of the Manor House, together with the gatehouse and the chapel above it. We then go through the house to the great tower and the structures around it, then out through the wide carriage arch at the south end of the Manor House and out through the gatehouse and down the long barbican in front of it. The tour

then proceeds from the pele yard and follows a course clockwise around the outside of the castle walls to the mill.

OUTER WARD

The open area in front of and to the east of the Manor House has been excavated archaeologically to expose the low walls of long-ruined buildings; their foundations are now marked out in the grass. It is here that the evidence for the early occupation of the site was found. During the heyday of the castle this was the public area for business and ceremony.

Great hall

The north side of the ward was occupied by the great hall of the castle **2**. The remains now to be seen represent a large building of the late fourteenth or early

5

*Outer ward. On the left is the site of the great hall. In the far corner was the kitchen (**4** on the plan). The east tower and site of the brewhouse are to the right*

fifteenth century, about 60 feet long and 46 feet wide (18 by 14m), constructed against the curtain wall. Its foundations along its south side extending down the centre of the ward are massively wide.

The great hall was a single storey building open to the roof; a hint of its magnificence comes in the remains of two windows with seats in the north wall. These windows themselves would have provided splendid views across the Tyne. At the eastern end of the hall was a two-storeyed cross range. The lower room **3** probably had a service function but on the first floor was a residential chamber with a latrine (garderobe) in the curtain wall. The thickening in the south wall of the hall was for external stairs to the first-floor room. A kitchen existed further to the east **4**.

This hall was replaced towards the sixteenth century by a smaller version to the west which was probably associated with the medieval residential range now incorporated into the Manor House. The line of this hall's thin south wall and the gable wall to the east are superimposed

over the earlier building. There are windows in the north curtain wall which suggest a first-floor chamber block at the west end of the later hall.

Other buildings of the outer ward
At the eastern and lower part of the outer ward are the fragmentary remains of several structures of various dates and floor levels which are likely to have been

*Site of the brewhouse in front of the east tower. Note the water trough and the fire-reddened base for the brewing vat (**5** on plan)*

East tower from the outer ward (**6** on plan)

service buildings—kitchen and bakehouse relating directly to the main function of the hall. A sixteenth-century brewhouse **5** was built immediately in front of the east tower **6**. It contains the fire-reddened base for the brewing vat and a stone water trough.

Moving round to the south, against the eastern side of the gatehouse was a late medieval two-storied stone building **7** which appears to have been divided into two on the ground floor. Both floors had latrines added which were contrived in the thickness of the curtain wall and discharged through a shoot on to the top of the bank outside.

The line of the gable for the pitched roof can be seen on the side wall of the gatehouse. This structure may have served as lodgings or as some form of administrative building. It is the last of a long sequence of buildings in this position.

Curtain wall

The curtain wall was built, rebuilt and repaired at different times since the mid-twelfth century. There has been a long history of instability because of its construction on and over the first earth rampart, especially on the north side. Most of the present openings in the wall (windows and latrines) relate to structures that have been built against it. The exception is the door to the rectangular east tower (also known as Watch Tower).

Stockdale says that in 1586 the tower was in utter ruin and decay. As it stands, its west wall was largely rebuilt in the nineteenth century and, according to Sir David Smith, converted into a powder magazine and armoury, presumably as a precaution during the invasion fears of the Napoleonic Wars. It is not now open to visitors.

Gatehouse

The gatehouse **8** is among the earliest visible elements of the castle and belongs to the early twelfth century. It is a simple structure built in coursed squared blocks of sandstone with round-headed arches to the front and back. On the outer side the arch has two orders with a square impost (block on which the foot of an arch rests) continuing as a string course (horizontal band of masonry) across the front and above a steeply sloping base. Above the arch is a second string course.

The gates were secured by means of a timber drawbar, the sockets for which remain in the jambs of the archway. The surviving medieval gates have been removed for repair and safekeeping.

The inner face of the gatehouse has two rings of voussoirs (wedge-shaped stones forming part of an arch) with a third arch above. Within the gate passage is an intermediate arch carried on corbels (projecting stone supports) in the form of pairs of grotesque heads.

The external steps on the western side lead to the chapel which was later built over the gate passage.

*Gatehouse from the barbican. The site of the drawbridge is in the foreground (**18** on the plan) dviding the barbican*

Gatehouse and chapel. The sanctuary is in the oriel (projecting bay) in the wall of the chapel

Chapel

The upper storey of the gatehouse **8** was converted to a chapel in the thirteenth century. At the head of the restored steps is a small porch at the chapel entrance, roofed with stone slabs.

The chapel has narrow pointed lancet windows, two in each long side and a fifth in the southwest angle which allows flanking cover along the curtain wall to the west. It is remarkable for the sanctuary which projects beyond the eastern wall face as an oriel (recess with a bay window). In the eastern wall of the projecting bay are two lancets above the site of the altar, while a third is in the southeast side in a position which allows the approach to the gatehouse to be covered.

A large pointed arch in the east wall separates the sanctuary from the remainder of the chapel. In the right-

The chapel with the sanctuary in the oriel beyond the arch. Changes made when the upper floor was inserted can be seen

hand jamb of the arch is a mutilated cavity which may be the remains of a piscina (basin with a drain). Below the arch two stone finials (decorative topmost features) are on display. One has pointed-headed panels, the other, unusually, has traces of human faces on each of the four sides.

Wardrobe

Probably late in the fourteenth century, an additional storey was added above the chapel to create a room known as the Wardrobe. This was for keeping archives and valuables.

The construction of this upper storey had the effect of lowering the height of the chapel and blocking the crenellations (indentations) in its parapet. The blockings in the south and east walls show externally but internally it is possible to see them more clearly, with the rebates for internal shutters, after the conversion of the crenels as cupboards.

The Wardrobe had embrasures with crossloops (narrow cross-shaped openings) for defence. There was a fireplace in the northeast corner now defined by a stone beam across the angle, though nothing else survives in the reset masonry. Externally, there is a late fifteenth-century battlemented chimney. The wardrobe was reached by a continuation of the external stairs.

By 1586, Stockdale describes the Wardrobe as covered with lead but in great ruin both in lead and timber. Restoration in the early nineteenth century was particularly heavy handed.

Steps to the chapel in the gatehouse and, above that, to the Wardrobe and battlements

*Gatehouse and the Manor House with the bow-fronted northern end on the right. The carriage archway (**10** on the plan) leading to the inner ward is on the left*

As well as the battlemented upper courses, the large iron straps with cross terminals and internal tie-bars are especially obtrusive. The cross terminals are, however, an attempt to evoke the crosses which are a principal element of the Umfraville coat of arms.

MANOR HOUSE
Dividing the inner ward from the outer ward is the Manor House **9**, built about 1808. It is a modest building architecturally, with Gothic elements particularly in the windows. The bow-fronted northern end has windows which give fine views across the Tyne to the north. The house still retains some of its internal decoration. The ground floor is occupied by exhibition rooms and the shop. The upper floor is the custodian's residence and is not open to the public.

This building replaced a late thirteenth-century residential range with subsequent late medieval alterations. The earlier building did not extend as far to the north as the surviving one. The later house was also wider, with its thick spine wall incorporating the western side of the medieval range.

By the end of the sixteenth-century this was a two-storeyed range. The lower floor had a great room through which there was a communication between the outer ward and the great tower. At its southern end was a chamber called the "parlour," and at the north end a little buttery (store room for food and ale). On the upper floor were two rooms called the "Utter Chamber and the Inner Chamber." From the outer chamber was a passage to the great tower by way of a first-floor gallery. From the inner chamber there was a passage to the chapel and on the other side a connection to a now-demolished building called the "Nursery."

When standing outside the chapel with your back to the door it is possible to see the remains of the gable wall and a fifteenth-century three-light window belonging to the medieval cross-range.

The inner ward and back of the Manor House showing the carriage archway with the gatehouse on the right

The blocked doorway in front of you, beside the gable window, is the door which provided communication with the chapel. Other traces of medieval walling with details of windows, doorways and fireplaces have been recorded in the walls of the Manor House, but almost all these features have now been plastered over during the course of returning the interior to its nineteenth-century decoration.

INNER WARD

It is possible to enter the inner ward **11** through the carriage archway **10**, between the gatehouse and the Manor House, or by going through the house and continuing past the stairs at the back of the hall and into the room to the left.

Here a tall round-headed arch opens on to an area which has been named the forebuilding **12**. The door on the left leads to a spiral staircase (not open to visitors); that on the right to a vaulted room now housing a display. From the forebuilding double doors through the east wall lead into the ground floor of the great tower.

Great tower (Keep)

This tower **13** is small when compared with other Northumbrian keeps such as those at Newcastle or Norham. Nor is it a self-contained tower house such as Bowes Castle in County Durham. It suggests a first-floor chamber within a strong tower which originally may have had a hall, perhaps in timber, alongside.

The unlit ground-floor space may have been for storage.

Internally, the tower measures 24 by 20 feet (7.3 by 6.1m) with walls 10 feet (3m) thick. It consisted, at the outset, of only two main storeys, as the scar of the line of the pitched roof on the inside of the west wall indicates. There would have been a wall walk and parapet masking the roof, and perhaps corner turrets as well. The additional upper storey and turrets which give the great tower a more traditional castle profile were built in the fourteenth or even early fifteenth century, but now only the southwest turret remains.

Externally, the early tower has shallow clasping buttresses at the angles and intermediate pilaster buttresses surviving in the middle of the south and west walls. Significantly, there are no projecting buttresses on the north wall, which suggests that if there was an adjacent hall structure or forebuilding this is where it could have been. It is also where the ground-floor entrance into the tower is located.

On the outer wall face on the south and west sides is a narrow horizontal string course of slight projection and a chamfered offset course above that. The only other early feature is the narrow round-headed loop lighting the stairs in the thickness of the west wall.

The masonry in the lower parts of the tower is similar to that of the gatehouse—comparatively small, roughly square blocks of sandstone. It seems likely that the tower and the gatehouse belong to the first half of the twelfth century but are not necessarily contemporary. Later refacing used larger more oblong stones, while the early nineteenth-century masonry refacing is very apparent, here as elsewhere, having a pronounced clawed finish.

The ground floor level in the tower has been raised. The room was originally entered from the doorway in the north wall, the threshold of which is now buried. The other doorway, cut through the east wall, is considerably later in date. The tower was not vaulted; the joist holes for the timber floor partly survive in the north and south walls. The roof structure was carried on projecting corbels.

Access to the wall top was by stairs within the west wall (these can be seen from the base of the curtain wall steps in the inner ward), approached by a passage in the north wall. It is possible that the tall round-headed arched window recess in the north wall was once a first-floor entrance into the tower before being converted to a window. A small mural chamber was approached from the western reveal but this opening was later blocked. Otherwise there are no surviving early features. This is because much of the south and east sides of the tower is missing, and a great part of the remaining north wall was refaced at a later date.

The tower was drastically altered in the late fourteenth or early fifteenth century, possibly after the castle's acquisition by the Percy family. The removal of a structure against the outer face of the north wall may have been the occasion for the substantial alteration of this side of the tower. It involved the insertion of a two-light window in the suggested early first-floor entrance and the blocking of the door to the mural chamber.

The introduction of an additional storey to the tower produced another large domestic window in the north wall, similar to that below. This and the raising of the wall tops with battlemented corner turrets above meant a revision of the internal communications. A wide spiral staircase in the rebuilt southwest corner

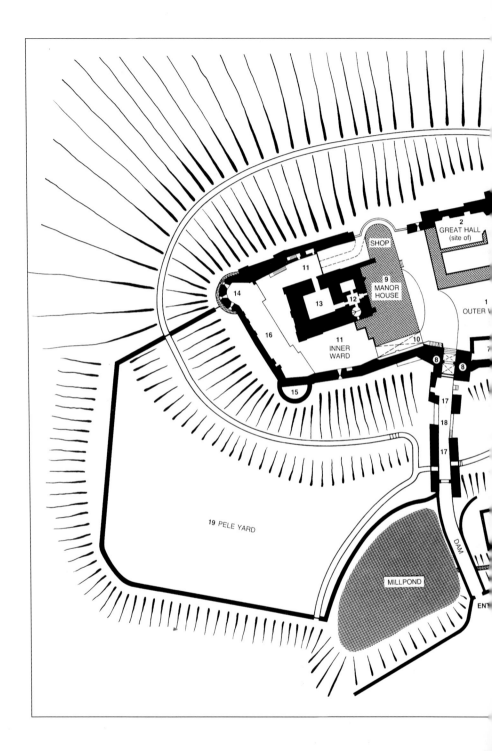

2
GREAT HALL
(site of)

SHOP

11

9
MANOR
HOUSE

14

13

12

1
OUTER W

16

11
INNER
WARD

10

8

8

7

15

17

18

17

19 PELE YARD

DAM

MILLPOND

ENT

PRUDHOE CASTLE

Tour plan

1 Outer ward
2 Site of great hall
3 Site of service room
4 Site of kitchen
5 Brewhouse
6 East tower
7 Site of medieval building
8 Gatehouse, chapel above
9 Manor House
10 Carriage archway
11 Inner ward
12 Forebuilding
13 Great tower
14 Northwest tower
15 Base of southwest tower
16 Conservatory, stables and carriage house
17 Barbican
18 Site of drawbridge
19 Pele yard

The numbers above and on the plan refer to the Descriptive Tour

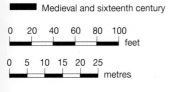

■ Medieval and sixteenth century

0 20 40 60 80 100
|___|___|___|___|___| feet

0 5 10 15 20 25
|__|__|__|__|__| metres

▲
– N –
|

Stairs within the west wall of the great tower

of the "forebuilding" abutting the tower gave access from ground to wall top by way of mural stairs in the south wall of the tower, but without direct access to the first floor. These stairs also had narrow lighting loops which cut the string course of the south wall.

Forebuilding

The great tower may have had an adjacent structure, perhaps in timber, against its east side as well as to the north, but early in the thirteenth century a narrow masonry domestic range was built against the east side of the tower. This range is known by the misleading description of "forebuilding" **12** (the name applied to a fortified extension of a

keep, covering external stairs and the first-floor entrance).

The junction of the two structures can be seen most clearly on the north side where the double chamfered plinth of the forebuilding can be seen to abut the plainer masonry of the great tower. At a higher level the masonry was bonded with that of the tower but only externally. The east wall of the forebuilding was subsequently incorporated into the outer (west) wall of the Manor House but the round-headed arch with a stopped chamfer in the eastern length of forebuilding wall and the chamfered plinth can be seen from within the later house.

At first-floor level of the forebuilding (not open to visitors) was the principal chamber, still retaining the remains of a decorative fireplace which formerly had a hood supported by stone caps to detached shafts which are now missing. This type of fireplace is unlikely to be earlier than 1185 and is probably later. Beside the caps are stone lamp brackets. The fireplace, in what must have been a room of some splendour, is at the same level as the floor of the great tower and the two rooms undoubtedly interconnected.

Much later in the thirteenth century, the domestic cross range, predecessor of the Georgian Manor House, was built parallel to, but detached from, the forebuilding. Between them was a narrow yard, but in 1586 Stockdale mentioned a gallery at its northern end connecting the two buildings. This arrangement could easily have existed from the outset.

Towards the end of the Middle Ages, the south end of the upper chamber seems to have been curtailed and the open yard (now glazed over) area between the two buildings spread into this part of the forebuilding **12**. The spiral staircase in a remodelled south wall has a late medieval square-headed door, and a window lighting the bottom of the stairs suggests that it looked into an open area. However, there is a passage off the stairs which leads to the forebuilding's first-floor chamber and there are traces of a roof line on the inner wall of the stair turret.

The vaulted store room at ground level (on your right when facing the double doors to the great tower) at the north end of the forebuilding, the door of which is opposite the doorway to the spiral stairs, appears to be quite a late development (perhaps even nineteenth century) and to have been constructed after the chamber above had gone into ruin. The top of its vault has no close relationship with the floor level of the chamber nor to the hearth of its fireplace. The doorway into the ground floor of the great tower may have been cut through at the same time.

The construction of the Manor House and other alterations and demolitions in this area, it has to be said, have made this an extremely difficult and complex area to interpret.

The two large thirteenth-century drum towers **14**, **15** on the western side of the inner ward and the site of a medieval building between them were sealed off in the nineteenth century to create a conservatory, stables and a carriage house against the curtain wall for the Manor House. These buildings **16** are now occupied as maintenance workshops and for the time being are not open to visitors. Only the base of the southwest tower remains but the shell of the northwest tower is almost complete. In the sixteenth century the southwest tower housed the garner (granary) with stables below.

In the northwest angle beside the northwest tower was a two-storeyed house which was in much decay in the

late sixteenth century. The roof line of this building can still be seen in the north wall as well as the steps and door jambs in the curtain wall.

Further along the thirteenth-century north curtain wall are external steps to the wall walk. On this side, opposite the ground-floor entrance to the great tower, is a door with steps rising to a latrine within the curtain wall, supporting the argument for a former residential building filling the space between the curtain wall and the great tower as late as the thirteenth century. Nearby is a ground-level door to a small room within the wall with no clear evidence for its function.

To the south of the great tower, but removed during the early nineteenth century, was a two-storeyed building known as the "Nursery." It was attached to the cross range and the lower portion of a window recess in the curtain wall may belong to it. This now contains a water trough, presumably associated with the later stables. The construction of the rear of the Manor House has removed all earlier structures.

The south curtain wall has a good example of an embrasure with a cross loop for a crossbowman. Many more can be seen from the outside. The instability of the rampart is greatly in evidence here with the pronounced lean to the curtain wall.

Leaving the inner ward by the carriage archway a grotesque corbel with two heads can be seen reset in the southern wall. It is similar to those in the gate passage.

THE EXTERIOR
The external appearance of the castle may be seen by returning to the gatehouse **8** and going out through the barbican, then proceeding clockwise round the walls to reach the watermill

and the dam with the pele yard beyond. In this way the defensive strength of the castle, its earthworks as well as its walls and towers, can be appreciated (see the aerial view on page 5).

Barbican
Immediately in front of the gatehouse itself is a masonry extension **17** which was clearly added much later, perhaps as late as the fourteenth century to give more forward protection and to house the bridge-lifting mechanism. There was no portcullis in front of the gate.

On the front of this low tower there are few architectural details surviving—a string course above a chamfered offset with stop-chamfered jambs to the gateway. In the west wall is part of a splayed embrasure for an arrow loop. This was much later cut through to form a doorway. Steps on the outside of the opposite wall show that another comparatively modern doorway had been inserted for access to the base of the rampart.

In front was the ditch which was formerly crossed by a bridge. The huge sockets for the horizontal timber members of the bridge can be seen at the base of the walls. It is presumed that some form of lifting bridge was provided and a beam socket high on the front of the building may have had some part in the arrangements. Modern masonry ramps now fill the site of the bridge **18**.

Crossing the ditch and extending beyond it is the barbican proper, perhaps built in the first half of the fourteenth century. Flights of steps in the thickness of each wall led to the wallwalks. On each side of the passage is a postern gate giving access to the pele yard to the west and the slope of the outer ditch to the east. The gate arches are round-headed with ribbed vaults in the wall thickness.

At the end of the western barbican wall

The barbican from the gate passage. The steps led to wallwalks. The millpond can be seen through the lower archway

is one jamb of a doorway and the springers of an arch which led to an attached building and presumably into the pele yard. Stockdale refers to this as follows: "without the same is a litle Turnepyke, and on the west parte a large gate rowme, where there hathe bene a passage into the Lodgeinges there scituate without the Castle (as is supposed) or to the Chappell there standinge."

Pele yard
The area known as the pele yard **19** lies between the moats and ramparts. Here was an outer gate which was ordered to be constructed in 1326, and which was in decay by the end of the sixteenth century. Within the pele yard stood the chantry chapel of St Mary which was founded in the early fourteenth century and no doubt there were other buildings

The castle seen over the inner moat from the pele yard. The northwest tower is on the left, the great tower and the base of the southwest tower are in the centre, and the gatehouse and barbican are on the right

such as barns and stables.

This was the favourite spot for topographical artists of the eighteenth and nineteenth centuries to make their representations of the castle and contribute to the longstanding attraction of the castle to visitors.

Towers and walls

The defensive strength of the castle is best seen from the pele yard. Although the original battlements are mainly missing, the line of large beam holes set below the parapet to take the timbers supporting the projecting hoards (fighting platforms) along the south curtain wall is distinctive. In the curtain wall are the loops for cross-bowmen. There are two levels of cross loops in the curtain wall between the northwest tower **14** and the site of the southwest tower **15**.

The southwest tower now only exists

as a battered base with a nineteenth-century wall closing the gap. The northwest tower stands to almost full height. It has three tiers of cross loops with an additional tier of fire provided from the merlons in the parapet. The loops are staggered at each level thereby producing a comprehensive field of fire.

Further round the circuit, beyond the northwest tower, there are the projecting turrets for the latrines serving the north side of the yard. The windows of the fourteenth-century great hall are visible and then comes a great thickening of the curtain wall with many changes of wall line and horizontal string courses. The complexity of this mass of masonry is because of the many phases of repairs arising from a serious structural problem, accentuated by the contrivance of stairs and latrines within the wall at this point.

With the swing of the wall line towards

Southern curtain wall with the great tower and the Manor House behind

the south, the two cross loops in the east tower **6** suggest a considerable strongpoint at this salient angle. Many lines of fracture and movement show in the masonry often indicating the site of former features. One such is the site of the early gate tower to the southwest.

As the curtain wall approaches the gatehouse another latrine projection appears. This has a wide, shouldered arch which was given a grill for security.

Close to the gatehouse and bonded with it is a length of the earlier stone curtain wall of the twelfth century. A longer stretch of twelfth-century curtain wall is on the west side of the gatehouse.

Mill and dam

The castle is approached over the dam on the east of the millpond that was created by the sixteenth century. Below the dam are the walls of the ruined millhouse, now without its wheel but with mill stones leaning against the barbican wall. There is a date stone of 1752.

A length of medieval masonry with a chamfered plinth in the face of the dam suggests that there was an earlier stone causeway across the ditch.

To the southeast of the entrance beyond the car park along the track, which was once the line of the road in front of the castle, is a medieval bridge crossing one of the denes. It has a steeply pointed arch on the south side and a round-headed arch to the north. The parapets are modern.

Site of the mill with millpond dam beyond

History

The south side of Prudhoe Castle in 1728 from an illustration by Samuel and Nathaniel Buck

Our knowledge of the earlier history of Prudhoe Castle has increased enormously in recent years thanks to archaeological excavations directed by Laurence Keen and Dr David Thackray (1972-81). These have demonstrated three main phases of structural development on the eastern side of the outer ward before the construction of most of the masonry to be seen there today.

By its nature, however, this evidence cannot be satisfactorily displayed and the levels at which the outer ward are laid out are those of the later Middle Ages.

Archaeological excavations

The excavations suggested that the first phase of occupation on the site belonged to the mid-eleventh century. On the hilltop there was an enclosure bounded by a timber palisade and containing traces of at least two timber buildings in that part of the enclosure examined.

The next phase represented dramatic change: the palisade was replaced by a massive rampart of clay and stones, and on the south side of the enclosure there

was a robbed-out feature within the rampart which suggested the base for a large tower, probably an entrance tower. The two earlier internal buildings seem to have continued in use and there were traces of a third building. The appearance of such a substantial defensive rampart indicates the emergence of a fortification of ringwork type, and probably represents the impact of the arrival of Robert d'Umfraville in the area towards the end of the eleventh century.

Phase three involved a complete remodelling of the castle, with the timber defences of the ringwork replaced by a stone curtain wall on a foundation of cobbles and the building of the lower part of the present gatehouse.

The earlier presumed entrance tower seems to have been left standing for a time on the line of the defences and the lower courses of a postern gate towards the northeast of the ward can be seen on the outside. Along the north side of the enclosure was a hall-like building, below the site of the later great hall, and a kitchen towards the east. The timber

21

building on the south side was replaced in stone in this period. This third phase has been dated to the early twelfth century, perhaps a response to the Scottish King David's devastating incursions and seizure of Northumberland at the beginning of the Anarchy in 1138.

Norman Conquest

The old Anglo-Saxon kingdom of Northumbria had largely disappeared as a political entity by the eleventh century. The Scottish kings attempted to incorporate it into their sphere of control and had invaded Northumberland unsuccessfully several times, but with the arrival of the Normans, William the Conqueror began the process of integrating Northumberland into England.

This was not achieved until after 1080, with the construction of a castle at Newcastle very much as its military base, and by the insertion of Normans into ecclesiastical and secular government. Even so, it was not until the capture of Carlisle in 1092, and the construction of a castle there by William Rufus that the Norman Conquest began to be fully effective in the north.

In what amounted to a second stage of colonisation, a line of baronies east of the Pennines running from the Tyne to the Tweed was established after 1100, of which Prudhoe was one. The intermittent attempts by the King of Scotland to claim and to seize the earldoms of Northumberland and Cumberland most notably in 1138 and 1173–74 remained a continuing factor.

Robert-with-the-Beard from Umfraville in Normandy seems to have been one of those granted land in the border areas. His descendants claimed that he was granted Redesdale, Northumberland, by William the

Conqueror by the service of keeping it free of robbers. Though the grant may actually have come during the reign of William Rufus, the archaeological evidence from Prudhoe "supports the view that Prudhoe was originally granted with Redesdale at the end of the eleventh century" (LJ Keen).

Scottish claims to Northumberland

The barony of Prudhoe was formally granted to Robert d'Umfraville by Henry I for the service of two and a half knight's fees. Nevertheless, the Umfravilles, as did others of the leading Northumberland families, had close connections with the Scottish court, particularly when the Scottish King held the earldom of Northumberland. Robert and his son, Odinel d'Umfraville I, who succeeded his father in about 1145, was a witness to several Scottish royal charters and his son, Odinel II, was brought up in the household of Earl Henry, father of the Scottish King, William the Lion.

Earl Henry held the earldoms of Northumberland and Cumberland following the peace settlement with King Stephen of England in 1139, and it was the reclaiming of the earldoms by Henry II upon King David's death, which caused bitter and lasting resentment in Anglo-Scottish relations for the next eighty years.

On a personal level, it was the rejection by Odinel d'Umfraville of his Scottish relationship and of his upbringing in William the Lion's father's household in favour of the English King which so incensed William and ensured that Prudhoe Castle would be besieged in 1173 and 1174.

Sieges of 1173 and 1174

The first historical references to the castle itself in fact relate to its successful resistance to these two sieges. The action was vividly described by the contemporary chronicler, Jordan Fantosme. In 1173 William the Lion, having realised that Newcastle was unlikely to be taken without the use of siege engines, turned on Odinel d'Umfraville at Prudhoe as an expression of his personal grievance.

As described by Jordan Fantosme: "The King of Scotland had his pavilions, his tents, and his marquees pitched there, and his earls and barons assembled, and he said to his noblemen; 'My lords, what shall we do? As long as Prudhoe stands we shall never have peace.' "

The Flemish mercenaries were all for attacking and demolishing the castle but the Scottish lords were disinclined to wait for a long siege and persuaded the King to move on against Carlisle. As Odinel was important to the English king, Henry II, he was granted £20 to retain knights in Prudhoe Castle in Henry's interest after this first attack.

In the following year, "King William now goes straight to Odinel, intending to take him by surprise and seize the castle: but the castle was newly provisioned . . . Odinel had settled some excellent men in the castle, making it such a fortress that I never saw better ones anywhere." Odinel was, however, persuaded by the garrison to leave the castle as he would be given short shrift if the castle was taken.

The castle was assaulted but Odinel rode off on "good brown Baucan" and raised a relieving force. The siege lasted three days without significant damage to the castle "but outside they have lost their fields and their standing crops of wheat and their gardens were stripped by their evil adversaries; and anyone who could think of nothing worse to do barked the fruit trees, thus working off his spite."

Instead of pursuing the siege, the Scottish army moved off to Alnwick burning and harrying as they went. The siege of Wark during this campaign, however, demonstrated that without siege engines the Scots were not to make progress against strongly defended castles. Indeed when a catapult was brought into action at Wark the first stone "barely tumbled out of the sling and it knocked one of their own knights to the ground."

Odinel and his force eventually surprised the Scottish King outside Alnwick. The King's horse was killed and pinned William to the ground. His capture and the rout of the Scottish army ended this particular episode.

Odinel subsequently received substantial compensation on account of damage by the Scots, but it is not clear whether this was applied to the castle structure. After the second siege, however, Odinel levied labour for the rebuilding of the castle implying that damage had been done.

Period of peace

After the capture of William the Lion, Northumberland enjoyed more than a century of peace with Scotland, though King John laid waste the lands of the rebellious barons who had recognised the Scottish King, Alexander II, as Earl of Northumberland.

Odinel had died in 1182 and his son, Richard d'Umfraville, joined the northern knights against King John and had his castle and lands forfeited. They were restored in 1217. Richard clearly had strong views on his importance and complained in 1221 that the building of Nafferton Castle, less than 3 miles away, was to the detriment of his own castle of Prudhoe. Nafferton was unlicensed by the Crown, and the sheriff was authorised to destroy it.

As part of the royal policy for reducing the number and strength of baronial

Prudhoe Castle as it may have appeared in the fifteenth century

TERRY BALL

castles, Richard himself was ordered to destroy his castle of Harbottle, high up in the Coquet valley. Here he argued successfully: "that the castle was usefully planted on the Marches of Scotland towards the Great waste" (Cheviot Hills).

Richard died in 1226 and was succeeded by Gilbert I whose son, Gilbert II, was a notable warrior in the service of Edward I in Gascony as well as Wales and Scotland. Gilbert II inherited considerable estates in Scotland as well as the title of Earl of Angus through his mother.

It would seem that the period after the sieges and through the thirteenth century was a period of considerable rebuilding and improvement at Prudhoe. One sign of this was the foundation of a chantry in the chapel of St Mary in the pele yard of Prudhoe Castle in 1300 by Gilbert II. It is this Gilbert whose military effigy is in Hexham Abbey. The inquisition on his death in 1307 mentions a deer park at Prudhoe and 120 acres (48ha) of arable land.

Scottish wars

There is a good deal of evidence for military activity around the castle during the Scottish wars in the early fourteenth century. In 1307, Robert d'Umfraville IV, with William de Ros were appointed to defend Northumberland against the King's enemies. Robert was taken prisoner at the battle of Bannockburn in 1314 but was ransomed the following year.

In 1316 Prudhoe was provisioned and the King granted Robert 700 marks to maintain a garrison of 40 men at arms and 80 hobelars in the castle. In 1325 Roger Maudit, who was appointed constable of the castle by Edward II during the minority of Gilbert III, was ordered to keep the castle provisioned and to retain five men at arms at the

King's expense, and in the following year he was ordered to construct a pele (probably a timber tower) outside the castle gates at a cost of 20 marks.

The devastation caused by the army of David of Scotland, before its defeat at the battle of Neville's Cross in 1346, caused a high degree of military preparation. As lords of Redesdale the Umfravilles used their castle at Harbottle as a prison. During the early years of the fourteenth century, Robert successfully petitioned the King to keep these prisoners at Prudhoe until Harbottle Castle could be repaired following damage caused by the Scots.

The Percys

Gilbert III died childless in 1381. As his widow had married Henry Percy, Earl of Northumberland, the castle came into the possession of the Percys on her death in 1398. After the Percy rising of 1403 against the King, Prudhoe fell into Henry V's hands.

In 1415 Prudhoe was granted to John, Duke of Bedford, but it was restored to the second Earl of Northumberland in 1445. There is no record of any siege of the castle during the Wars of the Roses when the castle repeatedly changed hands with the rest of the Percy lands. It was restored to the fourth earl in 1470 and so remained, serving as a residence of the earls until Sir Thomas Percy joined the Pilgrimage of Grace in 1536, and was subsequently executed. There are records of roof repairs in 1519–20 and in 1524–25 and so the castle was being maintained.

The Percy resistance to Protestantism meant that their lands and titles were once more forfeit to the Crown and for two years they were held by John Dudley, Earl of Warwick, later created Duke of Northumberland. In 1557 Thomas Percy recovered his estates by way of a grant from Queen Mary. Religion continued to dog the Percy's interests during the following century. Thomas Percy was one of the conspirators in the Gunpowder Plot and the castle was searched in case he was hiding there.

Sixteenth-century surveys of the castle

We are fortunate that two sixteenth-century descriptions of the castle survive. The first was a survey taken of the Earl of Northumberland's lands following his execution in 1537: "The castell of Prudhowe ys a verey stronge fortresse stonding opon an hill nye unto the towne of Ovynghame, havying a greate depe dyke rounde aboute hit, and a greate stronge dongeon towre in the myddle there of covered with leade, and ys somewhat decayed as in the coverying there of, so that hit ys estemyed the reparacions there of wyll amounte to xxli. And Sir Reginald Carnaby nowe occupteth as constable . . . ."

The second is a more lengthy and detailed description by William Stockdale which lists all the buildings within the castle, with their dimensions and functions.

Recent history

The castle continued to be manned. In 1617, the annual fee of the constable was £10 a year and the porter £3-0s-8d. Yet, during the late seventeenth century, the castle fell further and further into ruin

and by the end of the eighteenth century the southeast corner of the keep had collapsed. Still the survivals of feudal justice, the Courts Baron, were being held but from the seventeenth century they were at Ovingham, not the castle.

Between 1808 and 1818, the second Duke of Northumberland repaired the outer wall and the great tower while the rest of the ruins within the enclosing walls were swept away. This process was described by Sir David Smith: "The interior of the castle is somewhat altered . . . the ruinous walls of the Hall, Kitchen, Nursery, Garner and Stable are taken away—The dwelling house has been rebuilt and enlarged by continuing its northern end as far as the foundations of the north wall where it ends in a bow. The decayed square building between the Great and West Towers has been removed and a stable has been built between the last mentioned Tower and the former Garnor . . . the east tower has been converted into a powder Magazine and Armory and a new Garden has been made without the Castle between it, the mill pond and the western exterior ditch, comprehending the site of the old chapel."

In 1912 the ruins were cleared of vegetation and again repaired. In 1966 the castle came into the guardianship of the then Ministry of Public Building and Works, and is now managed by English Heritage on behalf of the Department of National Heritage.

Glossary

Barbican Outer fortification protecting a gateway

Buttresses Masonry projections from a wall or the corner of a building to give additional strength or to resist the lateral thrust of an arch or roof

Chamfer Bevelled or mitred edge, formed by cutting off the arris usually at 45 degrees

Corbel Stone or wooden projection from a wall to support a beam, etc; corbel table, a projecting course of masonry serving as a support

Crenellation Battlement or indented parapet consisting of alternating merlons (raised parts) and embrasures (indentations). A licence to crenellate was the equivalent of a permit to fortify a residence

Curtain wall Defensive enclosure wall often connecting one tower with another

Embrasure Opening in a wall, usually splayed internally, for admitting light or shooting through; also used as the equivalent of crenellation (opening in the upper part of a parapet; battlement)

Finial Ornament at the top of a spire, gable, arch etc

Hoards or **Hourds** Protected wooden platforms projecting from the face or top of a curtain wall (q.v.) or tower of a castle for defence of the base of the wall. They were supported on wooden brackets, the horizontal holes for which can sometimes be seen

Hobelar or **Hobblex** Light horseman

Impost Block on which the foot of an arch rests ; top of a wall below the springing of an arch

Lancet Narrow single-light window

with pointed head, characteristic of the thirteenth century

Loop Narrow vertical slit in a wall, deeply splayed within to increase the angle of vision and/or the amount of light admitted, through which defenders shot with bows and later guns, hence *arrow loop, gun loop*. *Cross loop,* loop in the form of a cross

Merlon Raised part of parapet wall between embrasures, sometimes pierced with a slit

Orders Series of recessed arches and jambs forming a splayed opening

Palisade Fence of strong upright timbers for the outer defence of a fortified site

Pele (peel) yard Palisaded enclosure; *pele tower,* small fortified tower

Pilaster Shallow pier attached to a wall

Piscina Basin with a drain in a wall niche near the altar, for washing sacred vessels

Plinth Projecting masonry at the base of a wall or column, often chamfered (q.v.) or with decorative mouldings. *Dressed plinth,* stone of plinth with prepared shaped and surface

Portcullis Iron-shod wooden grill suspended in vertical grooves cut in the stonework of the gate passage and lowered in front of the gate for additional defence

Postern Secondary entrance, or gateway in a wall, often concealed and normally at the rear of a building

String course Horizontal band of masonry projecting from outer walls of a building and usually moulded

Ward Courtyard or bailey

28